TOP TIPS:
GROWING FAITH WITH FAMILIES

Pauline Burdett with Ro Willoughby

Copyright © 2007
First published 2007
ISBN 978 184427 249 4

Scripture Union England and Wales
207-209 Queensway, Bletchley, Milton
Keynes, MK2 2EB, England
Email:info@scriptureunion.org.uk
Website: www.scriptureunion.org.uk

Scripture Union Australia, Locked Bag
2, Central Coast Business Centre,
NSW 2252
Website: www.scriptureunion.org.au

Scripture Union USA
PO Box 987, Valley Forge, PA 19482
Website: www.scriptureunion.org

The right of Pauline Burdett to be
identified as author of this work has
been asserted by her in accordance
with the Copyright, Designs and
Patents Act 1988.

British Library Cataloguing-in-
Publication Data: a catalogue record
of this book is available from the
British Library.

Printed and bound in Dorchester,
England, by Henry Ling.

Logo, cover design, internal design:
www.splash-design.co.uk
Internal illustrations: Colin Smithson
DTP layout: Richard Jefferson

Scripture Union is an
international Christian charity working
with churches in more than 130
countries, providing resources to bring
the good news about Jesus Christ to
children, young people and families
and to encourage them to develop
spiritually through the Bible and
prayer.
As well as our network of volunteers,
staff and associates who run holidays,
church-based events and school
Christian groups, we produce a wide
range of publications and support
those who use our resources through
training programmes.

INTRODUCTION

Hatches, matches and despatches! Families are forever changing. Children are born, grow up, become adolescents and then adults … move on and out … create new family units. But there's more to it than that! Families are also changing because how we understand them changes. Not that there is anything new about this process of change. Patterns of family life and childcare have altered through the centuries, stimulated by social, economic and political change. Shifts in health, employment and mobility have all played a part. The challenge to those ministering to families is to recognise and work with these changes.

The Church with its emphasis on relationships and caring has a calling to offer practical support and nurture to children and young people within their family contexts. Family members need support whatever their varied circumstances: coping with a disabled child, facing choices about schools, moving house, battling with a disaffected adolescent, exhausted by the arrival of a new baby, hit hard by redundancy, broken by divorce, crushed by bereavement.

Additionally, the family today comes in a variety of shapes and sizes: a single-parent family, a nuclear family, a blended family made up of stepbrothers, half sisters, a family with 'part-time' members, coming and going from college, an extended family of several generations – like the extraordinary Bucket family in *Charlie and the Chocolate Factory!*

We live in societies where things go wrong – sometimes as a result of deliberate disobedience or irresponsibility, sometimes simply because we live in a fallen world. So, there is no such thing as the model family. Not even in the Church. Christians mess up their family lives, too.

However, ministry to families must be a priority for God's people if God's kingdom is to be preached and experienced in our broken, relationship-starved world!

Churches need to more fully appreciate the strategic place of families in the growing of the Kingdom. This means not only reaching out to families in the community with the Good News of the gospel, but also supporting families already within the faith community, strengthening their role and helping them realise their full potential.

Working with families is inevitably risky, difficult – but hugely rewarding. True, many churches are inexperienced at working with whole family units and don't always get it right. But it's a learning process – learning from God and each other.

The good news is that many children discover the authenticity of the Christian faith when they see it lived out within the family. Faith is caught as well as taught – passed on from one generation to another. Christian parents, grandparents, godparents, aunts and uncles have a responsibility from God to nurture faith in their children. The Church has a responsibility to help adults with this challenge – not to take over but to support.

This booklet is far from exhaustive. But hopefully it will set you on an adventurous journey of encouraging parents to nurture the faith of their children, reaching out to families with the Good News about Jesus Christ and seeing your church itself become more and more of a family.

In reality…

A Baptist church recently decided to let children participate in the communion service as long as parents agreed and felt that their child understood. One couple told the Sunday group leader that they had no idea how prepared their son was. 'You know much better,' they said. 'You see him every week!'

The leader felt like replying, 'But you are his dad and mum and you are with him every day!'

WHAT THE BIBLE SAYS ABOUT FAMILIES

Christians want to live their lives guided by the Bible, in a way that pleases God. That includes the challenge of how we organise our family life. But what does that mean in practice?

The Bible was written thousands of years ago when structures of society were very different. In fact, different styles of family life and the relative status of men, women and children are assumed in the Bible. Abraham, for example, led a nomadic lifestyle where polygamy was acceptable: not a pattern the Church would recommend today. But principles of how God wants us to live are consistently found. How do these principles impact on family life and the Church's responsibility to families?

God did not make us to be alone. At creation God said, 'It is not good for the man to be alone. I will make a helper suitable for him.'(Genesis 2:18). God created man and woman and commanded them to have children. Intimate relationships are an essential part of being human. We are made to be in close relationships with others, the prime expression of this being the close personal relationship between a man and a woman who together produce children. Significantly, the core idea of family-like relationships is even present in the way we understand God as three persons intimately inter-related – God the Father, God the Son and God the Holy Spirit.

Think about...

To spend more time reflecting on what the Bible says about families, read the article on a biblical basis for family ministry on the SU website:
www.scriptureunion.org.uk/families

God made us so that family is our first experience of intimacy. We recognise that children are best cared for in this family context – and other vulnerable members of the community too: 'God sets the lonely in families' (Psalm 68:6).

Of course, all human relationships are damaged as a result of sin. The Bible is littered with examples of family relationships gone wrong – between brothers like Jacob and Esau (Genesis 25); between brothers and sisters like Amnon and Tamar (2 Samuel 13); between husbands and wives like Hosea and Gomer (Hosea 1); between fathers and sons like Eli and his sons (1 Samuel 2); mothers and sons like the mother of the disciples James and John (Matthew 20:20-28).

Jesus himself was in a human family with identifiable historical ancestry (Matthew 1 and Luke 3). He had a human father, a mother, brothers and other family relationships (for example Mark 3:31-32). Even these relationships were not necessarily happy or idealised ones. Mary suffered the slur of illegitimacy, which may have lasted all her life. It is possible she was widowed at an early age. When Jesus was very small the family were refugees (Matthew 2:14). There was no ideal upbringing for the God who came to earth to be one of us.

So, though we are made for intimate family relationships, the reality is that they are normally messy. It is only by God's grace that any family learns to cope with and grow through such challenges.

Family in the Old Testament
From early days, the pattern set down by God was that a man and a woman were to leave their families to create a new family unit (Genesis 2:24). That unit was to provide care for children. The extended family was always assumed, to be involved in bringing up children, choosing marriage partners and providing for orphans and widows. The family unit was also the means of passing on values. So children were expected to honour their parents (Exodus 20:12) and faithfulness in marriage was commanded (Exodus 20:14).

The family context also nurtured the practice of loving and worshipping God: 'These commandments that I give you today are to be upon your hearts. Impress them on your children. Talk about them when you sit at home and when you walk along the road, when you lie down and when you get up ... Write them on the door frames of your houses and on your gates' (Deuteronomy 6:6–9). Psalm 78:1–7 reinforces the importance of passing on faith and understanding about God. Significantly, it would seem that the task of passing on the faith was an important responsibility both for those in the family home and also for the 'gate keepers' or wider community. For us, this means that families need to understand their responsibility – supported by the wider faith community – for the spiritual nurture of their children.

Family as redefined by Jesus
The family experience of Jesus seems to call into question some accepted patterns of behaviour. At the age of 12, for example, he established a certain independence from his parents by answering his mother's anxious rebuke when they found him in the Temple: 'Didn't you know I had to be in my Father's house?' (Luke 2:49). Jesus had an allegiance that was stronger and higher than family loyalty. He recognised that discipleship meant putting God before all others (Luke 14:26), although he probably did not literally mean 'hating' family, as some translations of the Bible put it, but making God a priority. In other words, obedience to Christ is the only justification for ever acting towards family in a way that could be seen as disloyal.

Jesus saw the wider group of his followers as his family: 'Whoever does the will of my Father in heaven is my brother and sister and mother' (Matthew 12:46–50). He defined family loyalty not in cultural or biological terms but in the light of commitment to follow God.

This does not mean that Jesus advocated neglect of family. One of his last acts on the cross was to provide for his mother, setting an

example of extending family care, when he asked John to be as a son to his mother (John 19:25–27). It would appear that, in the early days of the Church, members of his natural family were prominent members of the Christian community.

Jesus demonstrated the importance of family but anticipated that the new 'Jesus family', the Church, would be as significant as the biological family. The Church's purpose was to emphasise obedience and commitment to God, with followers of Jesus together forming a new community.

Family in the New Testament

People in New Testament times lived in households, but because adoption and slavery were common, sometimes these were more like communities. Faithfulness in marriage within the Christian community was required because it was a reflection of Jesus' love for the Church (Ephesians 5:21–33; 1 Thessalonians 4:1–8). Respect within families was evidence of belonging to the Lord (Ephesians 5:1–4). The Church, Jesus' new family, cared for those in need (Acts 4:32; 6:1–4; 2 Corinthians 8:1–5).

Family today

So family units today need to be seen in this wider picture. What a challenge for the Church!

Covenants or promises, most notably in marriage, hold families together but not all family relationships are based on such a commitment. Parents make promises to each other but children do not choose their human family nor do parents or grandparents choose the character of their children! The church community itself is an association based on choice. A family may be part of a local church and at some point some – but maybe not all – individuals within that family will choose to commit themselves to what it means to belong to that particular church fellowship. Of course, not all children end up choosing to identify with their parents' faith, much to the sorrow of family members.

The Bible does not say much about this, since independence from family ways of believing and behaving was almost unheard of in those times. However, the pain of rejection when the son leaves his father in the Parable of the Prodigal Son (Luke 15) and his joyful return home some time later, offers comfort and hope to many.

Today, the framework of a father and mother committed to each other and to their wider family has become the prime unit for family life, whether or not parents have entered into marriage. Marriage contracts exist in a society which is aware of temptations to renege on responsibilities. These contracts encourage commitment and underline the importance society places on stable family relationships. But the Bible presents marriage as more than this. It is a reflection of the faithful and loving covenant relationship between God and his people.

A church needs to welcome all, while wanting to encourage long-term commitments and the keeping of covenant promises – for the wellbeing of children, if for no other reason. There are many stories of couples who have become part of a church family and, as a result of God's work within them, have decided to make a more formal commitment to each other in marriage as part of their growing relationship with God.

In this century, when family patterns are more dysfunctional, the Church is challenged to fill in some of the 'gaps' that have been created in family life, as well as doing as much as possible to prevent gaps occurring in the first place.

> **Think about…**
> How welcoming is your church to families whatever their shape? To think about the importance of marriage for the nurture of children, visit:
> www.scriptureunion.org.uk/families

2 WHAT YOUR CHURCH CAN DO FOR FAMILIES

Begin by looking at how your church's programme is structured. It may match one or more of the following broad types.

The church with groups based on age, gender or interest
Most activities are organised according to age, gender or special interest – groups dedicated to pensioners, adults, youth, men, women, mums with toddlers, junior-aged children, music and so on. Occasionally – perhaps once a month or on special occasions – there is a family service mainly aimed at children and supportive family members.

The church which actively works in all-age settings
Regular or weekly all-age services are encouraged, ensuring that people of all ages engage in worship and learn together for all or part of the time. This is not a family service, targeted primarily at children, but worship that provides most activities appropriate for all ages.

The church which facilitates intergenerational worship
Structures are deliberately shaped to allow intergenerational groups or cells to flourish, enabling 'family' groups of all ages to meet on Sundays and through the week for worship, fellowship and outreach.

The church which focuses on relationships within a wide definition of family
There are many opportunities for people of all ages to be 'family' together throughout the week, such as family days, holidays, parties and activities within a service. Responsibility for children is not the only way of defining a family.

The church with a heart to serve the community
Volunteer involvement in the local community is encouraged,
particularly offering care and support to children and young people.
This may include parenting courses, surrogate grandparent schemes,
toddler groups, coffee shops, involvement in local schools. It may be
seen as evangelistic outreach and/or a means to offer support to those
who need it.

**The church which sees children as part of a wider family within
the community**
Your church recognises that all the children who attend events or
programmes you put on are not isolated individuals but active members
of a family. In today's multicultural society the size and influence of the
family and its community will vary.

CHURCH AUDIT

By completing the questions below, you will begin to explore family
ministry in relation to your church and community. This will help to plan
your unique approach to serving families and sharing Christ with them
both within your church and in your local community.

1   How would you describe your local community? For example, an
    ageing or a young population, urban or rural, a high crime rate or
    multi-ethnic, wealthy or poor.
2   What events or structures for supporting families already exist in
    your community and in other churches?
3   Does your church have a mission statement? If yes, what is it?
4   Describe the three most important things that define your church,
    such as passion for the Bible, outreach to children, pastoral care for
    the sick or elderly.

5 What activities does your church provide for parents and children (such as toddler groups, football, midweek clubs, Sunday school)?

6 How many families with children regularly attend church services?

7 How many children attend services/activities with grandparents/godparents?

8 Make a list of families the church has less immediate contact with. For example, church families with young children will be friends with other families; families who have recently had their child baptised; families contacted through holiday clubs.

9 How do you usually keep in touch with these families?

10 How might you extend that contact through building relationships?

11 How many new contacts have you made this year? under 5s and their parents; children (5–10); young people (11–18); dads.

12 What particular things would you identify in your building and programmes that make families feel welcome and at ease? in the worship area; in the main worship service; in your weekly programme; in your community activities.

13 Think about the environment in which you meet, including any constraints that it places upon you. Dream dreams; what would you love to see happening in your church, with and for families?

Think about...

To discuss your findings or to explore family ministry further, contact: Pauline Burdett, Scripture Union Family Ministry Project Manager, email paulineb@scriptureunion.org.uk

HOW TO MINISTER TO FAMILIES: STARTING POINTS, PRACTICAL STEPS AND FUN IDEAS

1 SUPPORTING FAMILIES WITH NEEDS

All families need support at some stage or another. But as many people do not live close to members of their extended family, traditional support networks for childcare are reduced. For generations, churches have been involved – and continue to be involved – in giving the kind of care and support traditionally available from the extended family of grandparents, aunties, brothers and sisters and so on.

New births

The arrival of a new baby is one of life's challenging events! Church-based new baby groups meet a genuine need and are often recommended by the health visitor. But there are additional ways where the local church can provide specific Christian input:

- Many parents are open to think about the meaning of life and the values they will pass onto their child, although fathers are only likely to realise this *after* the birth of the baby.
- After the baby's arrival, a church could offer to pray with a new family in their home, as one of the 'services' provided by the community.
- Many parents who are not married see the baby's christening or thanksgiving as a public statement that they are committed to be together as a couple. A sensitive christening or thanksgiving can demonstrate that the church is welcoming those who are seeking God, even though the parents may not fully recognise that themselves.

- Some churches create a 'cradle roll' and run an annual cradle roll service, linked to the toddler group.

Other times of transition

Moving house, choosing or changing schools, redundancy and bereavement are other times of challenge for families.

Some churches run a forum when choices are being made locally about secondary transfer. Services for families whose children are starting school for the first time have proved to be well attended by mums and grandparents. Parents and students moving to secondary school or university welcome support and prayer from the church.

Churches often seek to help all family members when there is a death in the family. Some, especially those who have many funerals or a bereavement ministry, include in their programme an annual service to remember people who have died in the previous year. A card is sent to the bereaved on the anniversary of the death.

Carers and toddler groups

Many adults caring for young children (mums, dads, grandparents, childminders, au pairs and nannies) feel isolated and lack adult conversation and company during the day. By joining a carer and toddler group, they can meet others in similar situations to relax and chat, share experience of the highs and lows of childcare, ask for help in an informal setting as well as having time and space to play with the children. The children have access to a wider range of toys than at home and begin to develop socialising skills. Activities such as stories and singing not only provide a shared experience but remind carers of half-forgotten favourites to repeat at home and can introduce the Christian faith gently through simply-told Bible stories and songs.

Family crisis centres

Many church-based initiatives provide for families in crisis, whether short or long-term. These include a drop-in for the disabled, pregnancy counselling, debt advice, practical support for the homeless. Directly and indirectly, these initiatives support families with care and expertise as well as demonstrating the love of Christ in action.

Helping dads relate to their children

Many men have not benefited from a positive role model from their own father. Additionally, many fathers – dads who are not in a stable relationship with the mother of their child, single parent fathers, male carers … in fact, any dad! – are confused by society's changing expectations of what fathers should and shouldn't do. *Who let the dads out?* is a programme initiated by the YMCA and promoted by

In reality…

In Chester a fathers' parenting course was trialled, looking at what it means to be a father and how to make fatherhood a priority. Over a dozen dads came and commented afterwards that they had never talked like this before with anyone. Most of them were outsiders to the church.

In reality…

Most fathers drop their children off at sporting events and activities, returning to collect them again at the end. But the YMCA Dads & Lads programme encourages dads, father figures and mentors to get onto the pitch with their sons and daughters and join in the fun! See page 31 for contact details.

Care for the Family that involves churches giving time and space for dads and their toddlers to come together for fun activities and, as often as not, bacon butties!

In reality…

Pat's husband had left her with two children. She joined a church and was delighted when several men in the congregation took her ten-year-old son to football practice every Saturday morning. This became the best part of his week.

Children's clubs

Holiday clubs and midweek clubs create many contacts with the families of children who come along. In developing your programme, consider how family members who don't usually come to church can be involved – such as by helping in practical ways like craftwork or serving refreshments. You could also run specific events for parents alongside the club, such as seminars on aspects of parenting or preparing children for transfer to secondary school. When families come to celebrate the holiday club in a closing event or an end-of-term presentation at a regular club, there is an opportunity to demonstrate what else the church provides and to pass on something of the message that has been communicated to the children. *Wastewatchers*, SU's holiday club programme for 2007, includes plenty of ideas for this, with a training module on the *Wastewatchers DVD*.

Many people who run midweek clubs make it a priority to visit the homes of the children regularly, if only for a few minutes, which underlines the church's recognition of the children as part of a family unit.

In reality…

'We began weekly visiting, building up good one-to-one relationships with parents. As well as frequently holding conversations on the doorstep, we've got involved with all kinds of things – advising children with homework, discussing parenting strategies, helping a single parent move furniture, supporting a family facing eviction, praying for people and exploring the Christian faith. Average weekly attendance at the club doubled.

Family, youth and children's worker in Chatham

Being surrogate family
Many parents living away from their extended family feel isolated. Their children miss out on regular contact with grandparents, aunts and uncles. This is especially keenly felt when a new baby is born or there's a family crisis. Many churches help out with food supplies or supermarket vouchers. But a 'surrogate family' is just as vital as practical support. Older women helping in a toddler group are a

wonderful source of such support, helping to identify situations of need traditionally met by the extended family.

2 SUPPORTING FAMILIES IN NURTURING FAITH

How can churches support families in worshipping together, maturing in their faith, and in passing on faith from one generation to the next? It won't happen by accident; it has to be planned and the church has a part to play in this. Children need to see genuine faith as an integral part of everyday living. But many parents do not know how to communicate their faith to their children; they need encouragement, role models and resources.

Encouraging parents to share their faith

Parents who have not grown up in a Christian environment or who had an unhappy childhood may have particular struggles about sharing their faith with their children. This may be especially so if one parent in the family is not a Christian or it's a single parent family or a blended family with a diverse set of expectations and relationships.

Think about...
The section on what the Bible says about nurturing faith is relevant here. Look back to page 7.

Churches can do the following:

- Provide opportunities – in a small group setting or coffee morning or even as part of a service – for parents and grandparents to share with one another, ideas they have had or picked up from books or conferences and also talk about God-conversations they have had.
- Recommend relevant books for parents and exciting Bible story books to read aloud to children.
- Purposefully provide subsidised Bible reading resources to help parents mature; and subsidised Bible reading publications for the children.
- Change the emphasis of Mothers' Day to be a focus on those who are 'spiritual' parents.
- Encourage parents to want, expect and pray for their children to come to trust in Jesus for themselves. Just making this a regular prayer topic will raise the profile of faith sharing!

Providing good role models

Many young people lack strong male or female role models. Celebrities held up by the media are often poor examples of the patterns we would want to provide for children, especially adolescent boys.

Many parents wish for alternative role models for their children. Churches are ideally placed to provide regular opportunities for young people to encounter good adult role models in a safe environment. With the permission and acceptance of parents, older church members can be encouraged to develop mentoring or 'uncle'/'aunty' roles with young people, with regular face-to-face contact, email and texts.

Parents also need role models. Opportunities both formal and informal could be provided for those with experience to pass on their wisdom in a way that inspires, not condemns. All parents, if they are honest, know that they haven't got everything right.

In reality...

When David's family moved to their new church, he was already part of a local scout group so did not join the midweek youth group. No-one in his Sunday group befriended him. Overnight, being part of church became a miserable experience. For months a man coming up to retirement made a point of talking with him at the start or end of each service. It was nothing special – just one adult taking the initiative to show interest in a young person. David went on to become an enthusiastic member of the youth group.

Working with children in their family context

All children live with others and those in church working with children need to be constantly conscious of this, especially if the children are on the fringe of church life or their families are part of other faith communities. Relationships and trust can be built by making home visits before a children's club begins, by inviting the family to pop in and see what is happening or by having a sharing time at the end of a week-long holiday club. When taking home memory verses or activity sheets, children can be encouraged to talk to their families about the activity and discuss what they think. Children's workers do not always find it easy to relate to parents or family members and this may be an area where training or support is needed. For more details on the implications of building relationships with families of other faiths see *Top Tips: Welcoming children of other faiths* (SU).

Parenting courses

These are proving to be hugely popular, both for those within the church and as a means of outreach. Discussion groups for parents, giving support and advice, are an invaluable way for parents to explore and voice their own needs and to receive wisdom. Sometimes these run in homes, in church or on school premises – during the day or in the evening. See page 31 for relevant websites. Group material to explore *Families with Faith – Survival Skills for Christian Parents* (SU) is on the SU website.

Protecting family time

Recent research from the USA indicated that up to the age of 11, it was the time a mother spent sharing faith that significantly nurtured her child's relationship with God. But between the ages of 11 and 14 it was the father's input that was far more determinative as to whether his child became a lifelong follower of Jesus.

Many churches deliberately cut down on programmed activities to allow families more time and quality time together. Maybe a parent needs to be released from a particular responsibility in church to have time for children or elderly parents. Could people without immediate family responsibilities be encouraged to take on more?

On the other hand, many Christian parents are so busy doing non-church leisure activities that they may pass on to their children the view that 'church' is just another hobby, for when there is no better option. Most Christian communities still meet on a Sunday, a day now seriously affected by its deregulation. Of course, there are many activities that can only be done on a Sunday (especially when parents are not together). But Christian parents need to be gently reminded about the faith messages they convey by the quality of their commitment to their local Christian community.

In reality…

Geoff was an elder in the church, which meant he was out several evenings each week and all Sunday. One day Ben, his 14-year-old, announced he wasn't going to church any more. Geoff made a decision that was seriously misunderstood by most people at church. He resigned as an elder, saying that he would not be at church on Sunday mornings. Instead, he and Ben would do something together. For six months they got to know each other, as they walked, swam or drove to places that interested them. Geoff was amazed at his son's many qualities. They talked about everything. Then Ben decided he'd like to go to church, so some Sunday mornings they went together. He told his dad, 'Now I know that I matter more to you than church. And I've seen first hand what your faith means to you.'

Making the most of mealtimes

Fewer and fewer families eat together; it's become a casualty of the many and varied commitments families have and our diverse patterns of living. But eating together is increasingly recognised as an excellent way to deepen family relationships and help children mature socially and emotionally. Mealtimes are opportunities for including non-family members in family life too. As we sit around the table and talk together, stories of faith can be passed on to the next generation.

Bible activity events

A Bible activity event can be organised for any time of the week with the aim of encouraging families to read the Bible and pray together. The programme is built around engagement with the Bible material in family groups – everything from storytelling to prayer, worship, games, drama and Bible memorisation. You'll find suggestions for putting on these events at www.scriptureunion.org.uk/families

Providing resources

A well-maintained church library or regular book reviews in services help parents know about the many available resources. Scripture Union publishes Bible reading guides for people of all ages. Some of these come in packs so that churches can buy them more cheaply to give away. There are many wonderful retold Bible story books and prayer books for parents to use

Top Tips: Growing faith with families

with their children. Also worth mentioning is Scripture Union's *Family Activity Organiser*. For more details see page 32.

Believing grandparents and godparents

In many families, the grandparents are Christians, but their children have dropped out of church involvement. These grandparents long for both their children and grandchildren to know God. Some churches make prayer for these families a priority, recognising the importance of those of grandparenting age in passing on faith. Godparents can have similar opportunities.

Many grandparents are deeply distressed by the fact that they rarely see their grandchildren because of marital breakdown. Churches can offer sympathetic support in such circumstances. One of many useful websites is www.childrenneedfamilies.co.uk

3 REACHING OUT TO FAMILIES

Any church that prioritises families will be in touch with people who do not yet know Christ. Serving the community through a ministry to families will open up all sorts of opportunities. Make sure the church leadership is fully supportive of any families initiative, and that it's backed up with prayer.

Making church family-friendly

Life is pressured and family life is busy, especially at weekends. Many people have to work on Sundays. Some sporting activities focus on Sundays for key match fixtures. Separated parents, step families or blended families often have to deal with 'access' times on Sundays. Family visiting these days often involves long travel times. Busy work schedules often mean that chores such as housework and shopping are squeezed into a Sunday. To all these competing claims on time, there is the cultural leap that many have to make to enter a traditional church Sunday service. Has your church thought about how you could become truly more family-friendly?

Intergenerational church

Good intergenerational worship takes place at a time that best suits people in the community – whether that's Sunday afternoon, Saturday morning, in an after-school slot or as part of wrap-around care. If possible, choose a time when there is no special reason for people to rush to get away at the end, to allow relationship- and community-building. Flexible timings means there's no possibility of a harassed parent feeling guilty about arriving 'late'. While being Bible-centred, engagement with God's Word can be creative and 'multi-sensory', using, for example, clay, bubbles, water and paint, music and visual stimuli. Language used in liturgy or worship should be child-friendly without compromising on meaning.

> **Think about...**
> The Child Friendly Church Award scheme was created following a review of its work by the Anglican Diocese of Liverpool. For more details, see www.liverpool.anglican.org. Also, visit www.familyfriendlychurches.org.uk.

All-age Sunday services

A good all-age service is far more than a service for children! It could include aspects of the intergenerational activities suggested above, or may be more traditional. Foundational activities include: opportunities to worship God and pray together; Bible-related activities that engage people of all ages and those with disabilities; interactivity, suitable for

In reality...

A good example of an intergenerational service is called 'Sanctus 2nds' which takes place on the 2nd Sunday of every month at a church in Manchester. The layout is café style, with small tables and chairs as well as adult-sized ones. After an opening liturgy and either a story, film or activity, people of all ages spend up to half an hour exploring three 'spaces': creative space (where something is made); café space (with newspapers, tea, coffee and an activity such as a wordsearch or quiz); prayer space (a range of multi-sensory prayer activities). For more details visit www.sanctus1.co.uk

different learning style preferences; a welcome for those on the 'fringe' of church; a chance to catch up on news and develop a sense of belonging to and care for one another as a 'family'; a place for safe and respectful relationships to develop across age groups.

In reality...

A church in Macclesfield moved the main service half an hour later to run an earlier 35-minute storytelling service for parents and young children. This took place in the newly-carpeted area of the chancel. The whole church got behind the idea being prepared to change their centuries-old tradition of service timing. Mothers from the toddler group came who would not usually come to church.

Mother's and Father's Days

A church with an active families ministry will take full advantage of the family-oriented days that occur in the calendar – while at the same time being sensitive that these are not necessarily happy days for those without a family or whose family experience is a sad one!

Family holidays and events

Church holidays and weekends can be expensive but are a great way for families of all ages and shapes to get away together and share experiences. Organised holidays such as Spring Harvest or Northern Lights make it possible for church groups to be away together without having all the burden of organisation, as well as encouraging people to meet Christians from other churches. Days or half days away can achieve something similar on a cheaper scale – a trip to a local farm or swimming pool, karaoke night, fish 'n' chip supper, film night, Sunday breakfast.

Christmas and Easter

Both these festivals provide opportunities for special events and outreach. Some churches run a short, fun, interactive Christmas Eve service timed for when the shops close, with mince pies and coffee. People come with their shopping, loads of kids, visiting aunts and grandparents. One church ran a Christmas lunch for single mums which included a manicure or massage as a treat.

Think about…
Make a list of all potential
family contacts that could be
developed and then note down
all the opportunities throughout
the year to share the good news
of Jesus – carol services, nativity
plays, toddler services, seasonal
craft events, Advent, Christingle,
New Year's Eve, Harvest,
Valentine's Day, Shrove Tuesday,
alternative Halloween… Try to
match them up.

*Celebrations Sorted, Christmas
Wrapped up!* and *Easter Cracked* (all
published by SU) contain bags of ideas
for seasonal fun activities.

Extended schools
The new extended schools initiative
being encouraged by the government
provides exciting opportunities for
churches to engage with the local
community and provide genuine support
to families. Possibilities include running
breakfast or homework clubs on school
premises, giving holiday care or
community-based parenting advice.
There is a delicate balance to be
achieved between providing supportive
care outside of the home and enabling parents to perform their
parenting roles within the home.

TEN TOP TIPS

- Consistently look for ways to make church inclusive and welcoming for all ages and for all families of whatever shape.
- Make prayer for ministry to families a priority for the whole church.
- Avoid being judgemental of varied and messy patterns of family life, recognising that God can transform relationships – starting with us – which will affect all other relationships.
- Actively encourage parents, grandparents and godparents to share their faith with children and young people (see Deuteronomy 6) – by providing good role models, resources and mentoring. And allow space within the church programme for these activities to be encouraged.
- Keep the Bible and the way it challenges us to love God and others at the top of the agenda in all you do in your families' ministry.
- Value the contribution to church family life of single and/or older people.
- Make the most of the many opportunities a church has to mentor and offer positive role models which strengthen family life and nurture the faith of younger family members.
- Be alert to the opportunities for partnership with initiatives by government, education and wider society, particularly at times when they engage with events or rites of passage in the family experience.
- Remember that God has called his people to bring his good news of forgiveness and wholeness to a broken world.
- Take risks and be imaginative! You can't do everything and you won't do everything perfectly – but you can learn fast, especially with God's Spirit within you.

RESOURCES

Further reading

Richard Patterson, *Families with Faith*, Scripture Union, 2007

Diana Garland, *Family Ministry*, InterVarsity Press, 1999

Philip Mounstephen & Kelly Martin, *Body Beautiful?: Recapturing a Vision for All-Age Church*, Grove Booklets, 2004

Mike Brossingham, *Building Family-Friendly Churches*, Methodist Publishing House

John Drane & Olive M Fleming Drane, *Family Fortunes: Faith-full caring for today's families*, Darton, Longman & Todd, 2004

Ron Buckland, *Children and the Gospel*, Scripture Union, 2001

Francis Bridger, *Children Finding Faith*, Scripture Union, 2000

John Hattam, *Families Finding Faith*, Scripture Union, 2000

Nick Harding, *Kids Culture*, Scripture Union, 2003

Michael Peplar, *Family Matters: A History of Ideas about Family Since 1945*, Longman, 2002.

Church of England Board of Social Responsibility, *Something to Celebrate: Valuing Families in Church and Society*, Church House Publishing, 1995

Margaret Withers, *Mission-shaped Children: Moving Towards a Child-Centred Church*, Church House Publishing, 2006

Family programmes and activities

Easter Cracked, Scripture Union, 2005

Christmas Wrapped Up! Scripture Union, 2003

Celebrations Sorted, Scripture Union, 2006

Annette Oliver, *Glitter and Glue: 101 Creative Craft Ideas for Use with Under-Fives*, Scripture Union, 2004

Kathy Cannon, *Pray and Play: 101 Creative Prayer Ideas for Use with Under Fives*, Scripture Union, 2004

Websites – offering advice, resources, parenting courses
www.scriptureunion.org.uk/families
www.ymca.org.uk
www.capuk.org (Christians Against Poverty)
www.sanctus1.co.uk
www.careforthefamily.org.uk
www.familyfriendlychurches.org.uk
www.childrenneedfamilies.co.uk
www.new-wine.org
www.parentalk.co.uk
www.familymatters.org.uk
www.positiveparenting.org.uk

Bible Reading
Scripture Union produces a wide range of publications to help people understand the Bible. You might like to request free samplers from our range of quarterly personal Bible reading guides for adults, young people and children. SOme can be bought in bulk to encourage churches to supply Bible reading material to families at a reduced rate.
To request a free copy or find out more:
phone SU's mail order line: 0845 0706006
email: info@scriptureunion.org.uk
fax: 01908 856020
log on to: www.scriptureunion.org.uk
write to: SU Mail Order, PO Box 5148, Milton Keynes MLO, MK2 2YX

FAMILY ACTIVITY ORGANISER

 Family Activity Organiser enables families to keep in touch with each other and keep in touch with God. Each week there is a column for each family member's activities and seven suggestions to help focus upon God together – story, prayer, puzzle, action, memory verse, concern for a world in need and church involvement.

FAMILIES WITH FAITH

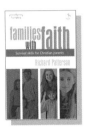 *Families with Faith - Survival Skills for Christian Parents* by Richard Patterson is a readable, warm and affirming guide that is strong on common sense and inspirational in its aim to put God at the very centre of family life. For more details visit www.scriptureunion.org.uk or your local Christian bookshop.